Car - ry the lad that is born to

O - ver the sea to Skye!

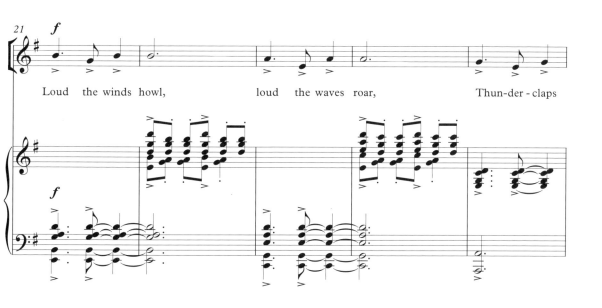

Loud the winds howl, loud the waves roar, Thun-der - claps

rend the air,_____ Baf-fled our foes stand on the

shore,_____ fol - low they will not dare, not dare.

dare._____

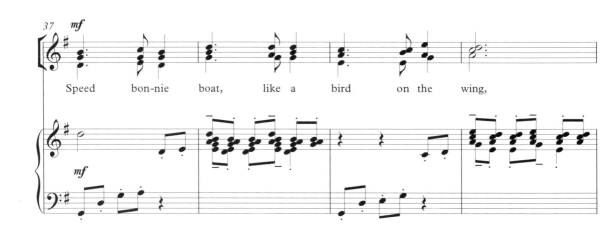

Speed bon-nie boat, like a bird on the wing,

for the BBC Last Night of the Proms 2005
and dedicated to the BBC Singers and the National Youth Choir of Scotland.
This version for the Inverclyde Junior Choir, for the BBC Last Night of the Proms 2006

The Skye Boat Song

Sir Harold Boulton
(1859–1935)

Scottish trad.
arr. **BOB CHILCOTT**

An orchestral accompaniment is available to hire from the publisher.

This piece is also available in an arrangement for SATB in *Bob Chilcott Songbook* (ISBN 978–0–19–335571–2).

OXFORD UNIVERSITY PRESS, MUSIC DEPARTMENT, GREAT CLARENDON STREET, OXFORD OX2 6DP

OXFORD

Carol Bowns

Secular

BC 92

upper voices (SSA)
and piano

Bob
Chilcott

THE SKYE BOAT SONG

On - ward the sail - ors cry!

Car - ry the lad that is born to be king,

O - ver the sea to Skye!

cry! _____ Car - ry the lad that is born to be king, O - ver the sea _____ to Skye!

Processed in England by Enigma Music Production Services, Amersham, Bucks.
Printed by Halstan & Co. Ltd., Amersham, Bucks.

ISBN 0-19-335671-6

9 780193 356719